MRS. EDGERTON

Personal from Meghan Cahillane

Father Serra: Traveler on the Golden Chain

Kathleen Allan Meyer

Our Sunday Visitor Publishing Division
Our Sunday Visitor, Inc.
Huntington, Indiana

Cover and Illustrations
Monica Watts
Design
Nancy Amor

Copyright © 1990 by Kathleen Allan Meyer

All rights reserved. No part of this book may be reproduced or transmitted in any form or by any means, electronic or mechanical, including photocopying, recording, or by any information or retrieval system, without written permission from the Publisher.

Send all inquiries to: Our Sunday Visitor Publishing Division
                           Our Sunday Visitor, Inc.
                           200 Noll Plaza
                           Huntington, IN 46750

ISBN 0-87973-139-7 (hardcover)
ISBN 0-87973-141-9 (softcover)
Library of Congress Catalog Card Number 89-63335

Acknowledgments

I am deeply grateful to the many individuals who have helped make possible this book about Father Junípero Serra. Special thanks are extended to the following for their assistance in researching this book: Jackie Boyden, my tour guide for twenty of the missions; Nancy Fortman, for our trip to Mission Dolores; Esther Cummings, Reference Librarian at Burlingame Public Library, Burlingame, California; Marge Harger, Children's Librarian at San Mateo City Public Library, San Mateo, California; Barbara Escofier, Branch Librarian at Foster City Public Library, Foster City, California; Ruth A. Smith and Nancy Jung of Foster City Public School, Foster City, California; and last but not least, two excellent listeners and critics, my good friends Katharine and Harold Guay of San Mateo, California.

To my daughter Leslie, who inspired me to write this book after our visit to the Carmel Mission.

Table of Contents

A Boy's Dream

Eight-year-old Miguel José Serra knew there was someone special coming to supper. His nose told him so. There was the delicious odor of *espinagada** rising from the kitchen hearth. And his mother had set the wooden table with her best pottery dishes.

He hoped the expected guest would be one of the Franciscan friars from the nearby friary. Then he could learn more about his favorite Franciscan, Saint Francis. And, best of all, the friar might tell another story about the New World and the native people who lived there and had never heard of God!

"How I would like to go there myself when I grow up," whispered Miguel to himself. He shivered with excitement just thinking about it.

A dream he often had began to creep into his thoughts. Someday he would become a missionary and leave his home on the Spanish island of Majorca. A tall ship would carry him through the sparkling blue Mediterranean waters into the dark, treacherous ocean. Then it would sail off to unknown lands. There he, Miguel, could teach the natives about God!

He had never even dared tell his mother and father about his dream. He was afraid they might tell him he could not go.

Still dreaming, Miguel washed his hands in the big stone basin. Little did he know that his dream was to come true!

He would be called Father Junípero, after a favorite companion of Saint Francis. And he would succeed in baptizing over six thousand natives so they

Note: For an explanation of this and other words and phrases, please see the glossary starting on page 57.

1

might follow God. They would help him establish the first nine Spanish missions along the coast of Nueva California, another name for Alta (Upper) California.

These missions would form a "Golden Chain"— the beginning of California's great and rich state!

On this journey he would encounter hardship, sickness, starvation, fierce tribal raids, and those who did not believe in him or his dream. None of these obstacles would stand in his way!

But let us go back to the very beginning of this story — the day, November 24, 1713, when his father, Antonio Serra, excitedly tacked a laurel branch to his front door in the little town of Petra.

"As you can see, good friends," he shouted, "it's a boy! Margarita has given me a son! He will be called Miguel José. Praise be to God!"

The Serras' first two babies had died. And now the proud parents were overjoyed that they had a new son.

"He is not a strong one," the midwife told them as she passed the baby over to the new mother. "And he will always be small for his age and weak, too."

Farewell to Petra

Miguel José Serra stood to one side as his classmates chose up teams.

"We can't use you, Miguel. Wait until you grow bigger, and your legs carry you faster," they called out to him.

This really came as no surprise to Miguel. He was always being told he was too short or not strong enough. And he would hear it over and over again in the years ahead.

But small as he was at eight years he hoed and tilled like a grown-up in his father's fields. Before going to the friary each day for his lessons Miguel also led the family's animals out to pasture. And his muscles strained and his young face turned red as he carried the heavy water jar back from the town well. His family needed a fresh supply each day.

Working side by side with his father little Miguel learned many things about livestock and farming. The crops they raised together were very similar to those he and his neophytes later would plant in Nueva California.

The climate on Majorca was ideal for raising olives, figs, lemons, oranges, artichokes, and almonds. Because of this Majorca was called "The Golden Isle." Years later, because of Father Junípero Serra's crops, California would be called "The Golden State."

But even more important to Miguel were his lessons. He was curious about everything. Much to the delight of the friars, he soaked up knowledge like a sponge.

After he learned to read and write and studied mathematics and religion, he asked to study music. He particularly liked the Gregorian chant, a type of singing.

He became very good at this. When he was eight, one of the friars invited him to chant with the other Franciscans on feast days. It did not matter to anyone that he was small for his age! He could chant much better than any of the bigger boys.

And with each passing day Miguel's longing to become a Franciscan increased.

Happy and secure, the young boy grew into teenage years. When he was fifteen, his parents decided to provide higher education for their very bright son.

"You shall go to the city of Palma and enroll at the university," they told him.

To Miguel the city of Palma must have seemed very far from home. It was a seven-hour journey over twenty-five miles of winding dusty roads to the southern coast. He had never before left his hometown, Petra.

He knew he would miss his sister, Juana, three years younger, and his parents. And what would he do without the good friars who always welcomed him into their midst, who gave him guidance and encouragement?

And would he be able to find his way on Palma's many streets? There would be no friends to help him. Miguel shivered in the coldness of the dawn as he wondered what lay ahead.

It must have been difficult for him to say good-bye to Juana that morning in September 1728. His father and mother would be traveling with him.

Miguel turned to wave one last time as he rounded the bend. Then he straightened his shoulders and looked ahead.

Already he was beginning to follow a rule that would help him make his dream come true. Twenty years later, when he left Spain never to return, he stated this rule in a letter to his parents: "Always go forward — never turn back."

"You're Too Short!"

Not long after they arrived in Palma, dusty and tired, Miguel José Serra's parents said good-bye to their son.

"You must apply yourself to your prayers and studies," cautioned his father. Then he and Miguel's mother, fighting back tears, walked away down the cobbled street.

The teenager tried to smile. A stranger, a priest of the cathedral, would now supervise him. But, even though he was already homesick, Miguel accepted his new life. This would lead to what he desired most — becoming a Franciscan.

A year later at sixteen Miguel applied to enter the Franciscan order. The priest in charge denied him admission, saying, "You can't be old enough, Miguel. You're too short!"

Finally the canon of the cathedral provided proof of Miguel's age. Then the young man became a novice in training and was kept busy each day from dawn till after midnight.

Since Miguel was too small and frail to do the heavy farm work he was told instead to clean stables and scrub floors. And imagine how foolish he felt when they discovered he could not even reach the lectern on the altar! The rest of the novices, on the other hand, could easily turn the large pages of the hymnal for the priest.

Miguel felt disappointed, too, that his parents were not allowed to visit him or even write to him. These were often sad and lonely times.

His consolation was reading about the Franciscan missionaries. He always requested his favorite book about Saint Francis, founder of the order.

"Do you have *The Little Flowers of Saint Francis*?" he often asked the convent librarian. Then he could read about Brother Juniper, whom he especially admired. Brother Juniper had a great sense of humor and was very devoted to Saint Francis. Miguel wished to follow in Brother Juniper's footsteps.

So it surprised no one when he chose the name of Fray Junípero Serra the day he became a Franciscan brother. After Miguel had taken his vow of poverty, a wonderful thing happened to him. It was almost like a miracle. He began to grow taller, and he also became stronger and healthier!

Now he was required to take more studies. He applied himself so well that he was made a teacher. Later he was ordained a priest.

While he was teaching, a young man named Francisco Palóu enrolled in his class. Neither of these men could foresee that they would be adventurers together founding Spain's "Golden Chain" of missions in Nueva California. Juan Crespí, another of Father Serra's students, would follow him there also.

One day Father Serra and Father Palóu discovered they shared a secret wish — to bring religion to the native tribes in the New World. During the next ten years they volunteered many times to go there. Their superiors said "no," pointing out that they were needed more at Palma.

Suddenly a new danger threatened the Spanish claims made in California many years before. Russia had moved into Alaska and its ships were advancing southward. Now Spain had to protect its claims.

Again the two priests asked to go to the new frontier, and again they were refused. Then one day a messenger arrived from Cádiz saying that some of the missionaries had run away. They had seen the small ships and great waves, and they were afraid. Now the king of Spain needed others to take their places. At last the Father Guardian agreed that the two priests must go. They were overjoyed!

Father Serra preached his last sermon at the little parish church he had been baptized in. Then he said good-bye to his elderly parents. Should he tell them they would never see him again? Father Serra decided to say farewell in a letter sent from the port of Cádiz, where he would board an English ship.

When the little ship sailed out of the harbor bound for Málaga, it was a sad moment for Father Serra. He might never see his homeland again. And yet there was happiness in his heart, too.

He was now on the first leg of the journey to make his lifelong dream come true!

Perilous Journeys

Little did the two priests know that extreme danger awaited them on board the English ship. It would be twelve long days before they were safe once again!

The captain, crazed by drink and his dislike of Spaniards, argued about religion day and night. Father Junípero Serra defended his views with Bible verses. This made the captain so angry he threatened to throw the priests overboard.

"Our king will demand indemnity from your king and you will pay with your head," calmly replied Father Serra.

The night before they landed, the captain, dagger in hand, approached Father Serra. He placed the weapon at the priest's throat but fortunately did not harm him. That was a sleepless night for Father Serra and his friend Father Francisco Palóu.

After a stay of five days in Málaga, the priests had an uneventful voyage to Cádiz in southern Spain. But the next part of their journey across the Atlantic was again perilous for another reason.

A month after the two Franciscans sailed for Puerto Rico, in August 1749, the drinking water ran low. Each passenger was allowed only a pint a day. All except one grumbled about the terrible heat and their thirst.

Like his namesake, Brother Juniper, Father Serra had a sense of humor. He told the others his own remedy: "Eat little and talk less!"

Once in Puerto Rico the Franciscans remained there for eighteen days. Then they set out on another perilous journey to Vera Cruz in Mexico. For most of the time the ship encountered good weather. Just before arriving, however, a violent hurricane buffeted the little vessel as though it were a toy ship.

Before long the ship began to leak, its pumps being all but useless. Then the ship's crew mutinied against the captain. They wanted the ship to be run aground so that at least a few could be saved.

Father Palóu wrote this account of it: "We had no recourse than to prepare ourselves for death. But our Fray Junípero, in the midst of that great storm, retained as undisturbed a peace and as tranquil a mind as if he were experiencing the most serene day."

He continued: "When he was asked whether he was afraid, he answered, 'A little.' But when he remembered the purpose of his coming, even this fear left him immediately."

The priests began to pray loudly to Saint Barbara. The great storm ceased soon after. And gentle winds blew the ship into Vera Cruz. The main mast was gone and the bottom of the vessel had huge holes. It was a miracle they had survived and they thanked God!

The last part of the journey was overland to the missionary training center at the College of San Fernando. Mexico City was still two hundred fifty miles away! At the king's expense, horses had been offered to the Franciscans. Father Serra refused to ride, as he wished to follow the example of Saint Francis, who never burdened his good friend, the mule.

Father Serra did not realize what rugged country awaited him and his companion, Father Pedro. Father Palóu was to remain for the time in Vera Cruz because he was ill.

At first all went well for the priests. One night, however, they came to a deep river. It seemed impossible to get across. In this wilderness someone suddenly appeared on the opposite bank. The stranger showed them where the river could be easily forded. Then he led them to his home, fed them, and provided shelter for the night.

Another time the Franciscan missionaries became weak and faint from lack of food and water. Again a stranger seemed to appear out of nowhere. He gave them a juicy pomegranate, and they were able to forge ahead.

Only one misfortune took place on this journey. But it would torment Father Serra for the rest of his life. Once, as he lay sleeping, a mosquito bit him on the left foot. The foot swelled and became infected. The open sore never healed.

There was no turning back, however. Fifteen days later Father Serra, in great pain, hobbled into Mexico City. He was now six thousand miles from home.

But the real journey as a missionary was only beginning for the little lame priest!

Attempted Murder

In spite of his infected foot Father Junípero Serra was eager to begin the strict training. Hard work, lack of sleep, and loneliness lay ahead. The priest would face these same conditions as a missionary.

He was assigned a bare cell, but he was there very little. Nights were spent mostly in prayer. Days were devoted to more prayers, saying Mass, and classes. In these classes the Franciscans learned how to organize and maintain missions. They also studied the languages of Mexico's native tribes.

There were lonely times as well. The priests were discouraged from talking to one another. Their only freedom was to walk briefly about the city but only after getting permission.

On these walks Father Serra saw how poor the natives were, and in contrast how wealthy the Spanish people were. The latter dressed in fine clothing and wore jewelry of gold and precious stones. The Franciscan knew that the gems and gold had been discovered by the natives of the area. He also disapproved of the Spaniards' dancing and singing in the streets all night.

When he preached, Father Serra spoke out against his countrymen's way of life. Many Spaniards disliked him for this, but he did not care. And he waited for the time he would be assigned to Mexico's missions in the Sierra Gorda.

Six months after his arrival that wish came true. And his best friend, Francisco Palóu, was also accepted! When it came time to leave, the two missionaries chose to walk. Father Serra's foot had improved, but during the next sixteen days on mountain trails it began to swell again.

The pain was forgotten when the Franciscans entered the village of Jalpan. The half-wild Pames tribe lived there. Father Serra tried to talk to some of them, but they did not understand him. Not one to give up, the little priest found someone to teach him their language. He stayed up far into the night practicing, and the Pames began to respect and trust him.

Because Father Serra realized that the natives could not easily understand the Church's teachings, he showed them the beauty of his religion by visual means. He kept the church building brightly lit up with many candles. He also made sure that flowers adorned the altar.

Moreover, he sent to Mexico City for a beautiful religious statue. Every Saturday night it was placed on a platform and carried through the streets. The natives walked alongside with lanterns. They loved these processions. And they enjoyed feast days with singing, dancing, and eating.

On these days Father Serra and the children put on religious mystery plays. As a child in Petra he had taken part in them. At Christmas they presented a Nativity play. The Franciscan priest was a special friend to the Pames children. They climbed all over him when he sat down to read a Bible story.

To help the natives grow food he sent for oxen, cows, sheep, goats, farming tools, and seeds from the College of San Fernando. He rewarded a successful harvest with blankets, clothing, and material. The patient little priest taught the native women how to spin, weave, sew, and knit.

Soon Father Serra gave the Pames their own parcels of land, oxen, and seeds. The men learned how to farm, make tiles and bricks, and do carpentry work. Father Serra worked side by side with them for seven years building a beautiful new church. It is still standing. What a strange sight it was for the other priests to watch the frail, lame little padre in torn habit help carry beams. He had been a dignified priest and learned scholar in Palma!

When the Spanish soldiers and their families tried to take away the Pames' land, Father Serra stood up for the natives. He made sure they were treated fairly.

In 1758, Father Serra was called back to the College of San Fernando. For the next nine years he preached all over Mexico.

On one of these journeys someone tried to murder the Franciscan priest. One morning before Mass someone put poison in the altar wine. Halfway through the service, after Father Serra consumed some of the wine, he became white as a ghost. His tongue became paralyzed, and he was carried from the altar and given oil, an antidote for the poison. Finally able to speak, Father Serra recovered enough to preach the sermon that evening!

"Always Go Forward — Never Turn Back"

Suddenly more important matters began to occupy Father Junípero Serra. The king of Spain appointed him *presidente* of the fourteen Baja (Lower) California missions. At last he would be going to California! But he was not a young man anymore. At age fifty-six surely he must have had second thoughts!

How would he fare in the barren, sandy wasteland of Baja California? Some dwellings were nothing more than earth-built cabins. Water to grow crops was scarce, and locusts ate what little did grow. And what about his poor health, especially his ulcerated foot?

If Father Serra had such thoughts, no one would have guessed. He was ready to go forward!

With his good friends Father Francisco Palóu and Father Juan Crespí among the expedition members, he traveled to Loreto, capital of Baja California. It was a bleak land, and many of the missionaries wanted to give up and return to Mexico City. But Father Serra's spirit rallied them. Yet many times his foot and leg were so swollen and painful he could barely stand.

A year later, in 1768, the lame Franciscan missionary's life took another unexpected turn. English and Russian explorers had again become very interested in Alta California. This forced Spain to start colonizing in that area. The Spaniards would begin with San Diego, followed by Monterey, which had been discovered in 1602 by the Spanish explorer Sebastián Vizcaíno. Father Serra of the successful Sierra Gorda missions was chosen for the gigantic task —

building a chain of missions, a day's journey apart, along the coast of Alta California!

The plan was for Father Serra and his Franciscans to make friends with the natives in this new frontier. Then they would all live together in little communities. The priests planned not only to teach them religion but how to plant crops and raise animals as well.

Weavers, tanners, and carpenters from Mexico City would come and teach their trades to the natives. Later on, colonists would join them in the pueblos. If enough came, the king of Spain would not have to worry about the English and Russians anymore. A "Golden Chain" of these missions would take care of that!

Father Serra was overjoyed to learn that he was now also *presidente* of Alta California. His dream had come true — to go where no other missionaries had been before. He and Mexico's inspector general, José de la Sonora Gálvez, who had been sent by the king, excitedly planned the four expeditions — two by land and two by sea. Captain Fernando de Rivera y Moncada, his soldiers from Baja California, and Father Crespí headed the first land party. Captain Gaspar de Portolá, military governor of California, and Father Serra were in charge of the second. Together they loaded the *San Carlos* and the *San Antonio*. Another ship, the *San José,* planned to follow.

The Baja California missions were asked to share whatever they could. Among the things they gave were seed, plant and tree cuttings, dried fruits, wine, grains, salted meats, religious ornaments, altars, vestments, and tools. They also supplied oxen, sheep, horses, and mules.

Father Serra made sure that shiny beads, bright cloths, and church bells were carried on the pack animals of his expedition. He knew the natives would love the pretty beads and cloth. And the bells would call them to church.

The ships left first. Then the Rivera-Crespí party set out on March 24, 1769. Captain Portolá and his soldiers followed a short time later. Father Serra was to catch up with his expedition on the trail. Both parties took along neophytes from the Baja California missions. They would help to build the missions and be interpreters for the natives met along the way.

Father Serra, the *presidente* of Alta California, stayed at Francis Xavier Mission on his first night out. Father Palóu was in charge there. The two friends greeted each other warmly. They knew this might be their last meeting, as a dangerous road lay ahead of Father Serra.

In his diary Father Palóu wrote: "When I saw him and his swollen foot and leg with the ulcer, I could not keep back the tears when I thought of how much he still had to suffer on the rough and difficult trails. . . ." He knew that his close friend could even die along the way. Father Palóu tried to persuade the little lame priest not to go. But it was of no use.

By the time he caught up with Captain Portolá, Father Serra could neither stand nor sit. Would the captain order him back to Baja California? Would he suggest that he be carried on a litter the rest of the way to San Diego? The priest did not want to be such a burden.

Captain Portolá noticed Father Serra's extreme agony. He tried to persuade him to go back. He said the ailing priest would hold up the expedition. The Franciscan responded, "Even if I die on the road, I will not go back. . . . You can bury me here."

Dangerous Times Ahead

As he lay on the ground Father Junípero Serra noticed a muleteer putting salve on his animal's sore leg. The medicine was made of crushed herbs and tallow. He asked the man to put some on his foot and leg. The next morning the swelling was down and the pain almost gone. It was like a miracle!

Once the little band of travelers crossed over into Alta California they began to have many adventures. For example, they were kept awake for four nights by a roaring mountain lion following them.

On another occasion a guide captured a native spying on the travelers. Through an interpreter the native admitted that his tribe planned to ambush the party and kill everyone. Father Serra gave the native some food and several necklaces. Then he was allowed to leave. As a result of the priest's kindness the Spaniards were not ambushed.

Another time more natives followed them and every now and then would surround the little group. Their bows and arrows were always in their hands. Suddenly all the men disappeared, leaving their women behind. Just as suddenly they reappeared with a mighty war whoop. Then the soldiers shot their guns in the air, forcing the natives to retreat. It was a nerve-wracking time for Father Serra and the others!

One day another tribe surrounded them. The natives wanted everything the travelers had. In his diary Father Serra wrote: "From me they wanted my habit; from the governor his leather jacket, his waistcoat, breeches — in short, everything he wore. [One of them] even pestered me quite a bit in an effort to obtain my spectacles. So I gave them to him." Little did he know the native was going to run away with them! It must have been a strange sight to see the little gray-robed friar limping here and there chasing after his spectacles!

Finally, on the first of July, the weary men glimpsed their first sight of San Diego Bay. The Rivera-Crespí party was waiting there. In celebration an exchange of gunshots took place. Cannon shots from the two ships at anchor also boomed out a mighty welcome. Imagine what a joyous time it was for Father Serra! His joy, however, turned to sadness when he learned that almost half the men had perished from scurvy. And how would this affect further exploration with so few men left?

After his men had rested, Captain Gaspar de Portolá headed north to find Monterey. But first he ordered the *San Antonio* back to San Blas for more supplies. Father Serra remained to found the mission. Using a very old map, Captain Portolá passed right by Monterey. He went far out of his way. Soon the winter rains set in. They drenched the members of the little expedition. There was no food left. On the way back down to San Diego they killed some of the mules and ate them.

Father Serra waited and waited for Captain Portolá and his men to return. The Franciscan missionary had had troubles of his own! But he had founded San Diego de Alcalá, the first of Spain's missions in Alta California. On July 16 Father Serra dressed up in beautiful church vestments of red and gold, then lit the candles beside the cross inside the crude brush shelter. Loudly he rang the bell hanging from a tree.

"Come and be Christians," Father Serra called out joyously. But not a native appeared. How disappointed he must have been!

Gradually the natives did come. They wanted the gifts of beads, figs, and raisins. They liked the padre's bright cloth. But they also had something else in mind. They began to steal everything they could. One night they paddled out in their tule canoe to board the *San Carlos*. The soldiers caught them cutting up one of the sails!

Soon the natives grew tired of the Spaniards' staying on their land. One day, when soldiers took food out to the ship, the natives attacked the little brush huts. Father Serra and another Franciscan by the name of Father Vizcaíno stayed hidden in one of the huts. When Father Vizcaíno raised the mat at the doorway to see what was happening, an arrow pierced his hand.

A few minutes later a servant boy with an arrow protruding from his neck ran into the hut. Father Serra watched in tears as the youth bled to death. Several others were wounded before the returning soldiers drove the natives away.

Finally the Portolá party arrived exhausted and starving. Father Serra was disappointed to hear they had not found Monterey. But he was not discouraged. There was always tomorrow!

Now there were more people to feed, and there was almost no food left. Where, Father Serra wondered, was the supply ship, the *San José?* No one could know that it had been lost at sea!

Captain Portolá felt that there was no hope left for the expedition. He decided that San Diego Mission would have to be abandoned to the natives and sea gulls. Upon hearing this news, Father Serra was very sad. They had come so far. They could not turn back now!

He pleaded with Captain Portolá to reconsider. The captain agreed to wait until March 19 for the ship to come. If it did not, they would all return to Baja California.

But Father Serra had an answer to that. "I shall remain here with Fray Juan Crespí alone to hold out to the very last."

March 19 was nine days away. The little padre organized prayers to Saint Joseph, the patron saint of the expedition. Anxious hours filled anxious days.

Late in the afternoon of the last day a lookout cried, "A sail! A sail!" Father Serra hurried to the beach. There on the horizon was the *San Antonio* loaded with supplies. Now everyone would stay and build the first mission of "The Golden Chain" together. And once more the little *presidente* would not have to turn back!

Forward to Monterey

And now another challenge lay ahead for the gray-robed friar. He must found a mission at Monterey by order of the king. Father Junípero Serra knew that some day Monterey might become the capital of Alta California and the headquarters for Spain's missions. Nothing, he told himself, must stand in the way!

Because of his infected leg the Franciscan missionary agreed to sail to Monterey Bay on the *San Antonio*. Captain Gaspar de Portolá and his party set out once again overland. Upon his arrival there, the captain realized that he had found Monterey Bay on the first expedition.

A curious sight greeted Captain Portolá as he approached one of the three huge crosses he had erected the winter before. The cross was surrounded by shellfish, mussels, and meat. These he felt were offerings to the white man's God.

Perplexed that the food was not eaten, the natives had then surrounded the cross with feathers and broken arrows placed upside down in the sand. This was a message to the Spaniards that they desired peace with them and their God.

Rounding the Point of Pines a week later, Father Serra must have been excited to see watch fires on the hills. It had taken him over six weeks to travel the four hundred miles from San Diego! The ship had been blown hundreds of miles off course. But he had no complaints except to say the trip was "uncomfortable." Impatient to get started, the little padre was standing in the prow of the first small boat ashore!

On June 3, 1770, Father Serra founded the second link in "The Golden Chain," Mission San Carlos Borromeo de Carmelo. The ceremony took place with great pageantry. The altar was built of boughs and brush under the same oak tree that Sebastián Vizcaíno's chaplain had held services in 1602. A parade of soldiers, neophytes, and sailors approached it from two sides. Resting upon the altar was a beautiful statue of the Virgin Mary given to Father Serra by the viceroy of Mexico, Antonio María Bucareli y Ursúa. The statue can be seen today at the Carmel Mission.

Cannons boomed and soldiers fired their muskets all during the service. Shortly after, Captain Portolá proclaimed the land as Spain's. Two months later, when the captain returned to Mexico City, a great celebration took place in honor of his founding the Monterey Mission. Special bells of the great cathedral could be heard throughout the city. All the other churches answered with their bells. How joyful Father Serra, the real hero, would have been to hear them!

Within a week he and Father Juan Crespí found the Monterey location not suitable for the mission. It did not have the three key requirements — water, good soil, and many natives nearby. Exploring the countryside, Father Serra discovered a site five miles away on the banks of the Carmel River. Now he would have to ask the viceroy for permission to move the mission away from the presidio. It would take months by messenger to receive an answer. It was difficult for Father Serra to be patient!

And little did the padre know his impatience would grow day by day now that Don Pedro Fages was the new governor. Captain Portolá had been understanding of the Franciscan missionaries' goals and needs. Governor Fages, on the other hand, had little interest in helping the natives and did nothing to prevent the cruel acts of his soldiers toward them.

This indifference on the governor's part brought about armed conflicts with the natives. As a result, many natives stayed away from the new mission and the later missions, much to Father Serra's sorrow. How would he ever attract the natives to the mission so they might become Christians? This was all the more reason why he needed to move his mission away from the governor's presidio!

Moreover, he and Father Crespí were not being treated fairly themselves! Governor Fages had built them a friary of plastered whitewashed palisades roofed with earth. But Father Serra did not appreciate his keeping the key to it. In a

28

letter the little priest revealed that it was "so as to lock us in and out when he pleased." Also, the door to their enclosure was built facing the interior court. The governor could then keep track of the Franciscans' comings and goings. In addition, their letters arrived with their seals broken. The little padre felt that some probably were never even delivered.

Most of the natives around the new mission were peaceful and docile, although they were often attacked by neighboring tribes while searching for food. In summer they existed mostly on berries, seeds, and pine nuts. In winter they had little to eat. Father Serra hoped to solve this by training them to plant gardens and raise cattle.

In the meantime, some of them started to come to the mission. And Father Serra joyously baptized a few, including a young couple's son.

To add to this joy, the long-awaited letter arrived saying the mission could be moved. Once on the Carmel River everyone turned to cutting down the big trees nearby. Unlike the mud-and-brush shelters built at San Diego, wooden buildings were possible.

A stockade fence of poles surrounded them. But the fence was not too secure at the top because of a shortage of nails. A new supply might not arrive for six months. Therefore, locking the heavy gate at night did not really keep the Franciscans and their companions safe from attack!

But Father Serra did not worry. He loved the location and even the cold, foggy climate of the Carmel Valley. Later, he would always say that San Carlos was his favorite mission. It was his home!

Two Missions in Two Months!

Even though he loved San Carlos, Father Junípero Serra knew he must move forward. Many more links were needed on "The Golden Chain."

And now he would be able to accomplish this! Ten padres had arrived unexpectedly one day that spring of 1771. To the little priest's joy they brought candles, incense, and bells for more missions. That night Father Serra showed the padres to their rooms in the crude friary as though the friary were a palace and they royalty.

Before long, however, he put on his dusty wide-brimmed hat, picked up his sturdy walking stick, and limped off. He and a small bodyguard of soldiers, natives, and two of the Franciscan missionaries were heading south of Monterey. They were in search of a suitable location for Mission San Antonio de Padua.

Five days later they came to a beautiful valley amidst the Santa Lucía Mountains. It was covered with oak trees, and a river flowed nearby. What a perfect place for another mission, thought Father Serra. It would be a most welcome sight in the wilderness for any travelers on their way to the San Diego Mission. Moreover, he had heard that the natives in the area were gentle and friendly.

Quickly the little party pitched camp. While some members unloaded the mule train, others helped the padres build a crude bell tower. Father Serra could hardly wait to ring the bell. He wanted its chimes to ring loudly across the countryside. Then the natives and the whole world would know he was founding another mission for God and the king!

The two padres accompanying Father Serra were amazed that the lame little priest should waste his energy tugging at the heavy bell. There was not a native in sight! But, as the new sound bounced off the mountains, it did attract someone!

A lone native boy suddenly peered at them from behind a tree. Father Serra was not surprised. Prepared for this moment, he pulled glass beads from his pocket. Cautiously he held them toward the boy. The native crept up silently and grabbed them. Then he quickly ran away. Imagine how pleased the little padre must have been!

It was not long before the boy returned with others. They laid seeds, wild grains, acorns, and pine nuts at Father Serra's sandaled feet. He was encouraged by their friendliness. Later a few natives requested that he baptize them and make them Christians. And they disclosed to the pleased padres where they had hidden their idols in the woods. They said the priests could destroy them.

The natives were very helpful in building Mission San Antonio de Padua, which was founded on July 14, 1771. They carried wood for the Franciscans. And they dug long ditches from the San Antonio River to bring water to the gardens. The irrigation system they built with its reservoirs and huge pipes were used many years later by ranchers. This mission was also famous for its water-powered grist mill that ground grain into flour. And the natives here became California's first farmers by growing fine orchards of fruit and olives.

In time San Antonio would prove to be one of the most peaceful and prosperous missions. Two weeks after its founding Father Serra set out happily for Monterey. He was already feeling very optimistic about its future.

His next mission, San Gabriel Arcángel, established on September 8, 1771, was not to be founded as happily or have as bright a future. To begin with, Father Serra was not given the opportunity to found San Gabriel. Governor Pedro Fages had not ordered an escort for him to travel there, so the Franciscan missionary was obliged to remain at San Carlos. In his place Padre Benito Cambón and Padre Ángel Somera would accomplish the task. With only a few soldier escorts and without Governor Fages they arrived at the selected site.

The mission was to be built on the Río de los Temblores, Spanish for "River of Earthquakes." True to its name, the area was shaken by four earthquakes the day the mission was founded! However, it was believed that the location was ideal, having ample water, rich soil, and a gentle climate.

Just as the expedition was about to make camp, arrows flew through the air. It looked as though the Spaniards would all be massacred! Suddenly one of the padres held up a painting of Mary, Mother of Jesus. The natives had never seen anything so beautiful! The arrows and war cries stopped. The natives crept closer to look at the portrait. Then they laid down their bows and arrows and ran away.

They returned shortly with food and necklaces. These they placed in front of the picture. The Franciscans knew the natives wanted to be friends now. This same picture that saved them hangs in the restored mission church of San Gabriel. It is over three hundred years old.

After that first day the natives were very willing to help the padres build the mission and also enjoyed planting its crops. The missionaries gave them kernels of corn and told them to plant them. Later the plants sprouted, and the natives called the corn "white man's magic." The priests also taught them how to plant prickly pear cactus hedges around their fields to keep the animals out. It took less time than building an adobe wall.

But, suddenly, all this peacefulness changed. Governor Fages now brought his men to the mission. He allowed them to make fun of the natives. And he did not discipline them when they were cruel even to women and children.

Finally, the soldiers insulted and hurt the wife of the chief. Led by the chief, the natives attacked the soldiers. The chief was killed. Then the natives really went on the warpath. The mission was almost destroyed.

This was a great tragedy not only for the natives but also for Father Serra and his missionaries. The tribe now distrusted the padres as well as the soldiers. They did not come back to the mission for a long time.

Problems Everywhere!

The *presidente*, Father Junípero Serra, had now succeeded in founding four missions in a little more than two years! There were two in the north and two in the south. He was getting ready to found another halfway between.

But the problem of supplying the missions had to be solved. If not, the mission system was doomed. Supply ships destined for Monterey remained in San Diego.

"Everything in San Diego, and nothing here!" Father Serra said sadly. He must persuade the captains to sail north. Governor Pedro Fages accompanied him on the trip to San Diego.

On the way there they left the coast and traveled inland to a lovely valley. Captain Gaspar de Portolá, on his first trip to find Monterey, had named it Valley of the Bears. He told Father Serra it had good soil and two streams running through it. But it was also inhabited by many grizzly bears!

A few months before the trip to San Diego, Governor Fages had come here on a bear hunt. The people of San Antonio de Padua and Carmel Missions were starving. From one hunt alone the governor took back nine thousand pounds of bear meat, some of which he gave to the natives.

The tribe was grateful but even more pleased that the bears had been killed. They had often been attacked by these fierce beasts. Their bows and arrows could not penetrate the fur and tough hides. Therefore, they welcomed the founding of Father Serra's new mission, San Luís Obispo de Tolosa, on September 1, 1772. They helped the padres and gave them seeds and other native foods.

Leaving the mission in good hands, the little padre continued on his journey. Now he was more determined than ever to ask the viceroy to remove Governor Fages because he had put so many obstacles in the padre's way as he planned for new missions. The governor had already said "no" to a sixth mission. And, after discussing the problem with the missionaries in San Diego, Father Serra was chosen to meet with the viceroy in Mexico City.

On October 17, Father Serra and his twelve-year-old native servant, Juan, sailed for San Blas. From there they set out on foot to cover the hundred miles to Guadalajara. Their journey took them through mountains and deserts. They arrived eight days later extremely ill. Now fifty-nine and very frail, with an infected foot and suffering from asthma, the little priest was believed to be dying.

Gradually, however, he improved. But the fever returned on the two-hundred-mile walk to Quereturo. Again he was given up for dead. This time he also believed he was about to die. His recovery a few hours later was like a miracle! He continued his journey to Mexico City, which was still one hundred fifty miles away. He arrived on February 6, 1773, too ill and weary to see the viceroy for several months.

The viceroy was very sympathetic to the ailing padre. He asked Father Serra to draw up a list of laws governing Alta California under the mission system. (In doing this Father Serra is recognized as the sponsor of the first body of laws to govern early California.)

This "Bill of Rights" protected the natives. Their control and education were to be left to the missionaries. If a native deserted a mission, he would be pardoned and not punished.

As for the missions, the viceroy ordered that supply ships should go regularly to Alta California, including the port of Monterey. More soldiers were to guard the missions. And, at Father Serra's request, these soldiers were allowed to bring their families and start colonies. The viceroy also promised they would come on a new route — overland from Sonora, Mexico. He further agreed that the missions of San Francisco, Santa Clara, and San Buenaventura should be founded.

Father Serra was overjoyed. At last he felt that he had a good friend to help him. Things would be easier now. But little did he know, as he set out for home in

September 1773, that the new governor, Don Fernando de Rivera y Moncada, would be as difficult to work with as Governor Fages had been.

Not long after arriving home in May 1774, Father Serra discovered how little the new governor would do for the mission system. Although there were now ample supplies of food and materials, Rivera postponed their distribution. The little padre did not have enough food or clothes for the baptized natives. He and Father Francisco Palóu, who had come to Carmel, cut up their old habits and shepherds' blankets and sewed clothes for the natives. How frustrating this must have been for the Franciscan missionaries!

For months the new governor delayed responding to Father Serra's simplest requests. And he would not grant the priest permission to found any new missions, especially San Buenaventura. He said there were not enough soldiers to guard new missions and mules to haul supplies to them. After much heated discussion, however, Governor Rivera agreed to the founding of San Juan Capistrano, between San Gabriel and San Diego.

Occupied with many problems, Father Serra sent Father Fermín de Lasuén and thirteen soldiers to raise the cross there on October 30, 1775. Eight days later Father Lasuén learned of a terrible disaster to the mission system. Natives had attacked San Diego Mission and burned it to the ground. Father Luís Jayme had been tortured and killed.

Fearing a similar attack, Father Lasuén ordered that the bells of San Juan Capistrano be taken down from the trees and buried. Then he and the others abandoned the new mission site and hurried to San Diego. It was not until November 1, 1776, that the Franciscans returned to actually rebuild the mission.

The attack on the San Diego Mission had occurred on November 4. Trouble had been brewing since early October. At that time Father Jayme had allowed two neophytes to take a day's trip into the hills. One was Carlos, chief of the village nearest the mission. On the way he and his brother robbed two elderly native women. Fearing punishment they fled shortly afterward.

All during October they had secretly gone from village to village asking other chiefs to join them in an attack on the mission. Father Jayme had even heard this rumor about the possible massacre. He refused to believe it because he loved and trusted the natives so much. He felt someone was lying. But the lie became a reality!

On the first night of the full moon the chiefs and almost a thousand warriors descended upon the little mission with war whoops and burning arrows. The brush roofs of the buildings were set afire. The blacksmith was killed, and the carpenter was mortally wounded. The others, including Father Vicente Fuster, two young boys, and three wounded soldiers, escaped into a little adobe building. Father Jayme went out into the open and spoke to the painted warriors. "Love God, my children," he called out.

Before he had even finished speaking, they pushed him into a gully. Then they tortured him and beat him to death with their war clubs. Later he was recognized only by his white skin.

It was almost a month before Father Serra heard of the tragedy. He was shocked and saddened. He knew, too, that this was a big step backward for his mission system. No one would believe in it any more! Could he ever go forward again?

But right now, he told himself, he must reach San Diego and help rebuild the mission. Governor Rivera ordered him to remain in Monterey, since he wanted to go alone with his soldiers to severely punish the attackers. And, if Father Serra were there, he knew the little priest would never permit that.

Finally, seven months later, the still-saddened Father Serra found a way to get there. He sailed aboard the supply ship *San Antonio*.

The Chain Grows Longer

It had been a nightmare just seeing his first mission in blackened ruins. Then came the disappointing order from Governor Fernando de Rivera y Moncada not to rebuild. The governor said, "Stop all work! The natives are planning a second attack. The *San Antonio* must leave the harbor."

Father Junípero Serra knew that without the ship's crew, rebuilding would go slowly. Could Governor Rivera have made up this rumor? The little priest suspected the governor did not care if the mission was ever rebuilt or any more founded.

Frustrated by Governor Rivera's actions, Father Serra sent a letter describing the situation to the viceroy of Mexico. The priest waited anxiously for a reply.

At long last, Father Serra saw a gray cloud arise far down the narrow trail leading to the San Diego Mission. Soon a lone horse with his rider clothed in dust galloped into view. The little lame man hurried to meet the soldier.

"Padre-Presidente, a message from His Excellency, the viceroy!" the rider said breathlessly. The answer had finally arrived. Would it be the right one?

Father Serra trembled as he reached for the official circular letter. This was what he had been waiting for since coming to San Diego.

The viceroy did indeed agree that San Diego must be rebuilt. He also ordered the founding of three more missions — San Francisco, Santa Clara, and the abandoned one, San Juan Capistrano. As for the natives guilty of burning San Diego, they were pardoned, much to the little priest's joy. Once again he could go forward!

A few weeks later a happy Father Serra set off to dig up the bells at San Juan Capistrano. But first he traveled to San Gabriel to get supplies for the new mission. He gathered together food, cattle, and neophytes. Always anxious to get started, he went ahead of the pack train. Only one soldier and a neophyte accompanied him.

Halfway there, they were surrounded by a large crowd of natives. In full war paint and with bows drawn they were about to kill the travelers. Suddenly the neophyte played a trick on the hostile natives. He told them, "The king's soldiers are following us. If we die, they will kill you!"

They lowered their bows. Then Father Serra blessed his attackers and gave them beads. He later told Father Francisco Palóu he thought it was the end of him.

Continuing on, the little Franciscan was barely able to sit in the saddle because his infected leg was so badly swollen. But he gathered strength upon arriving at San Juan Capistrano. He placed silver candelabras and sacred vessels on the wilderness altar. He tried to make the crude little chapel look like a cathedral. He believed that would entice the natives into the church.

A year later Father Serra would see the first section of an adobe church built at Capistrano. It is still standing today, the only one left in which the little padre celebrated Mass. It is the oldest building in California and is known as "Father Serra's Chapel."

In January 1777, the Franciscan missionary arrived at San Carlos. He heard wonderful news. The sixth link, San Francisco de Asís, had been forged on "The Golden Chain." And his dear friend Father Palóu had offered the first church service there on June 29, 1776. Little could Father Serra know that on the east coast of this vast continent the signing of the Declaration of Independence had taken place in Philadelphia just five days after that. What mattered to him was that this new mission at San Francisco honored his beloved Saint Francis.

To help found the presidio and mission the viceroy had ordered the explorer Juan Bautista de Anza to find safe trails from Sonora to Alta California. He was to bring families on this new route. First they would live at missions and later in pueblos.

On this second trip Anza brought two hundred forty colonists and soldiers and their families and about one thousand domestic animals safely to Monterey. It took them six months to come overland from New Spain, as Mexico and other parts of the New World were called then. Four babies were born along the way.

After choosing the site for the northern presidio and mission, Anza turned over the expedition to Father Palóu and a Spanish officer named Lieutenant Morago. They brought twenty-five families and five hundred cattle and horses. The site was near a stream that Anza named Arroyo de los Dolores, in honor of Our Lady of Sorrows. Today the mission is often called Mission Dolores rather than its official name.

They waited for Governor Rivera to arrive and agree to the building of the new mission. Finally they could not wait any longer for his approval and therefore went ahead with their plans. Later, in fear of the viceroy's disapproval of his delay in consenting to the new mission, the governor did agree to its founding.

On October 4, with the building under way, Father Serra and his companions decided to have a great celebration in honor of the feast of Saint Francis. A big parade was held. The statue of Saint Francis was carried on a platform. Later it was placed on the altar. All that day cannons boomed, soldiers fired their muskets, and colonists sang joyful songs. Little could any of those present, including Father Serra, dream that from this small settlement of tiny wooden huts with tule roofs would develop one of the most important cities of the Western world!

Again, fearing to disobey the viceroy's orders, Governor Rivera now agreed to found another mission at the southern end of San Francisco Bay. He and his soldiers and Father de la Peña traveled to Santa Clara. On January 12, 1777, a cross was erected. To Father Serra's joy this brought the number of missions on his "Golden Chain" to eight! The new mission was called Santa Clara de Asís after Saint Claire. It was the first mission named after a woman. Shortly after its founding, the pueblo of San José was formed nearby. Today it is one of California's most important cities.

Even though eight missions had now been founded, the years ahead would be filled with despair and discouragement for Father Serra. The first blow came when he opened an official letter from the College of San Fernando. As he read it the little priest slumped in his chair. It was a letter of disapproval and it took away many of his responsibilities. How would he be able to found any more missions? His title of *padre-presidente* no longer had any meaning. For the first time he felt defeated.

"Perhaps I should retire," the downhearted little Franciscan thought.

He was now sixty-five years old and not in good health. His asthma caused him severe breathing problems. And his ulcerated leg and foot made it impossible for him to walk at times.

Then he turned to prayer. Before long he had the answer. "I am not going to give up," he said determinedly. And he sat down to write a long letter to the College of San Fernando. Ten months later the governing board revoked their critical letter. His prayers had once again been answered!

In the meantime the viceroy sent Father Serra the happy news that the king had proclaimed Monterey the capital of both Baja and Alta California. Father Serra was grateful that the king recognized the work of the padres at Monterey.

The letter also informed the little Franciscan priest that a new governor, Don Felipe de Neve, had replaced Governor Rivera. Now, Father Serra thought, the mission system might go forward. But, almost from the beginning, the new governor had different views from the *presidente's* about founding new missions. He believed that pueblos rather than missions should be formed. He also said that the natives should live separately from the missions. Father Serra knew that the natives were not yet ready to live in towns. He could see that this would lead to the ruin of the mission system.

For five years no new missions were founded. Finally, on Easter Sunday, March 31, 1782, the little padre blessed the site of San Buenaventura, his ninth mission. He did not know it would be his last. The viceroy had ordered this mission be founded fifteen years before. But many obstacles had been placed in Father Serra's way.

Shortly afterward the Franciscan missionary traveled to Santa Barbara thinking he would found his tenth mission. Governor Neve did not tell him that he was going there only to start the military chapel at the presidio. When Father

Serra finally realized this, he left for home. The little priest was very ill and broken in spirit.

During the next two years, however, he continued to visit all his beloved missions twice more. No one could keep him from doing that!

"In California Is My Life"

These missions — this land called California — were Father Junípero Serra's life. He had told this to the viceroy and his Franciscan brothers in Mexico City almost ten years before when he bid them a sad farewell. Now, as he felt his life drawing to a close, he clearly recalled his words to them: "In California is my life, and there I hope to die." He had enjoyed the years in the Sierra Gorda missions. But other Franciscans had founded those. The nine missions in Alta California were part of him. They had fulfilled his dream. He had brought the word of God where it had never been heard before.

And someday he hoped there would be many more missions added to "The Golden Chain." Then they would be only a day's journey apart. And all the natives throughout California would be close to a mission. Many might become neophytes. He also envisioned that these missions would provide a safe haven for couriers and travelers at day's end.

Already each of the nine missions was different and yet alike. Each resembled a tiny town built inside a wall. In the beginning there were just small huts of sticks, mud, and branches. Tules formed their roofs. Poles were used for corrals and stockade fences.

Later the natives cleared the land for permanent buildings of adobe bricks and stone. The most important one was a four-sided building around a square. This was called a quadrangle. It had a definite pattern. The church was usually in the northeast corner. You could easily tell it by the large cross beside it. Bells hung nearby in a tree. Next to the church was a cemetery.

The other rooms surrounding the square, or patio, were the padres' and

45

visitors' quarters, the unmarried women's rooms, the kitchen, workshops for the natives, and storerooms. Outside the quadrangle were a few barracks for the soldiers, the natives' huts, and behind them the tannery, pottery, and weavery.

In order to construct the permanent buildings, the padres taught the natives how to make adobe bricks. Crushed adobe clay and wild oat grass were thrown into a hole. Then water was added to make mud. The natives jumped into the pit and mixed the mud with their feet. Hoisted up in leather buckets, the mud was poured into wooden molds each twenty-three inches long by ten inches wide and two to five inches deep. These shaped the adobe mud into bricks. Placed in the sun, the bricks became hard.

The men also learned how to make plaster and mortar out of limestone and seashells. These were used to waterproof adobe walls and line aqueducts. The Franciscans showed the natives how to divert water from streams by digging these ditches. Then water flowed easily to the mission and its gardens.

In addition to this the padres expected the men to work hard at other jobs. They plowed and planted the fields with many kinds of crops. They tended cattle, sheep, horses, goats, hogs, and chickens. Learning from the missionaries how to soak and tan hides and then make saddles, shoes, and ropes was another new job. Some men trained to be blacksmiths, carpenters, and tilemakers. Clay formed around half logs was baked in kilns for a long time. This made beautiful red *tegas*, which replaced the thatched grass roofs at the missions. These would not catch on fire from flaming arrows.

Women had many tasks, too. They were taught to sew, spin sheep's wool, weave, and make soap and candles. Household chores such as washing clothes and preparing corn and wheat to make bread and tortillas also filled their day. To the missions the natives brought the art of weaving beautiful baskets from reeds. These they used for carrying water, cooking, and storage.

Even the children were kept busy. They turned the adobe bricks so they might dry evenly. They chased birds away from the gardens and vineyards. The padres taught them Spanish and religion. And they learned to play instruments and sing in the choir.

The California missions would never have succeeded except for these

Horse Corral

Orchards & Fields

Tannery

Women's quarters

Weavery

Pottery

Indian Village

storerooms

Cemetery

Workshops

Sacristy

Bell Tower

Padres' Quarters

Nave

choir loft

Baptistry

Kitchen   Dining Room

Fountain

hard-working natives. Some historians criticize Father Serra and his missionaries for working the neophytes too hard. They also feel that the little padre's way of life was not right for the native Americans.

For thousands of years they had coexisted peacefully with nature — hunting, fishing, and gathering acorns, bulbs, and roots. They had worshiped their own gods and heroes. Singing, dancing, storytelling, and playing games made up an important part of their happy, easygoing way of life. Now this culture, even their gods, had suddenly been taken away from them.

On the other hand there are those who defend the mission system. They say that the natives were not forced to come to the missions. They came of their own accord because they wanted food, clothing, blankets, and pretty beads to wear. They wished to make their life better. And the padres sincerely tried to help them do this.

But critics of the system object even more to the physical punishment meted out to those natives who ran away to their former villages. Father Serra felt they were breaking a rule that was explained to them when they first came to the mission. Once they became Christians they could never leave the mission except for two weeks' vacation every five weeks plus days off for fishing and hunting.

The first time the runaways were caught by the soldiers they were given a good talking to. A second offense brought several days in the stocks. If it happened again, the offenders were put into shackles. And they had to work wearing the shackles. The fourth time they ran away, the natives were lashed with a leather whip.

Strict about punishing runaways, Father Serra would not stand for the soldiers' abusing the neophytes. The padres and soldiers were often in conflict over this. Proof of this was that the little priest ordered the Monterey and San Diego Missions removed from the presidios. What's more, he deplored the cruel things the soldiers did to the natives at San Gabriel and other missions. He complained often, but it did no good.

Before the missions were founded the Spanish crown told the Franciscans that they must not only Christianize the natives but also must train them to live independently. The idea was that the missions were temporary and would only be needed for ten years. At the end of that time the natives were supposed to be civilized enough to run a pueblo and take back their ancestral land. At this point, however, their culture was too primitive, and they were not yet ready to do this.

The padres were sincere in their training of the natives. They wanted them to have a better life than living in flea-infested huts and starving at times when their natural food was scarce. And they also wanted them to regain the land that belonged to them. Sadly this never came to pass.

Some historians also criticize the mission system for not protecting the natives from the white man's diseases, such as tuberculosis, measles, and chicken pox. Today thousands of their graves dot the foothills, deserts, and meadows of California. Prior to mission days the natives were quite healthy. They cured themselves by going to medicine men. They also used home remedies made up of herbs, berries, and roots. Of 4,771 adult natives baptized at Santa Barbara Mission the padres found only thirty cases of disease, lameness, blindness, and mental illness.

Some critics also say that the mission system was a form of slavery. At that time slavery was common all over the world. Thirty years after the missions closed, slavery still existed in the eastern United States.

With the coming of the Americans the natives found that they had been better off under the Spaniards. The Americans hunted down and wiped out whole tribes in their greed for gold and land that had belonged to the natives for thousands of years. The Yana tribe in north central California was one of these. Very little of this land either in California or elsewhere was ever returned to its rightful owners by the Americans.

Over two hundred years after the founding of San Diego de Alcalá there still remain two different points of view about the treatment of native Americans under the mission system. Were the natives treated unjustly? Were Father Serra and his Franciscans following the only possible plan there was to form a "Golden Chain" of missions over five hundred miles of wild and desolate country? Didn't working together help both groups of people?

This discussion more than likely will go on until the end of time. But now we will follow Father Serra on his final return to San Carlos Borromeo de Carmelo.

The Journey Ends

Exhausted and ill, the frail old man slumped on the back of the mule. He could see the gates of San Carlos Mission in the distance. Dust covered his worn, gray habit. The blazing sun had parched and cracked his lips. And the pains in his chest and swollen, discolored leg pierced his body.

But nothing mattered now. The five hundred miles of the slow and painful journey to bless his missions for the last time were forgotten. Father Junípero Serra was home! San Carlos Borromeo, his adopted home, was the place he loved best.

At times he had wondered if he would ever see his adopted home again. But there was no turning back. He must go forward. The end of his life was very close.

"God be praised!" the little friar whispered as he slid gingerly to the ground; "I can die in peace now."

Once home Father Serra stayed very close to his room. It was small and bare except for several crude pieces of furniture. There was a little table and chair and a low rush stool. His bed was a simple wooden frame covered with rough boards. A blanket covered the boards. At the head of the bed was his pillow. And always resting on the pillow was his big crucifix.

In the days that followed, the only time he left the cell was to limp painfully into church. It was just a hundred yards away. Once there his chest and leg pains were forgotten. Then he would enter the choir stall and sing joyously with his native friends.

He had arrived home in May, and now it was August. His condition was much worse. And he wanted to see his old comrade Father Francisco Palóu before he died. So many memories from long ago, both happy and sad, bound the two together.

How joyous Father Serra must have been to see his former pupil and companion again! Sometimes they sat on a small bench in the warm sunshine and talked of many things. Perhaps it was about the old days on Majorca and happier times.

Then the *San Carlos* arrived in the harbor. It carried supplies for all the missions. Dr. Juan García, the ship's doctor, came to see the little priest. He could neither help him get better or ease the pain.

Father Serra was more concerned about the rolls of cloth brought on the ship than about his health. He asked that the cloth be cut up and given to the natives. Then they could make warm clothing for the coming winter.

An old native woman came by as the two Franciscan priests sat in the sun one day. She asked for some cloth. Probably there was none left because Father Serra hobbled to his cell and returned with half of the blanket that covered the boards on his bed. The two padres recalled that she had come in the early days of the mission. Then she stole, killed, and ate the few chickens Father Serra was using to start a poultry business.

"Isn't she going to pay you for the chickens?" joked Father Palóu. In reply, Father Serra chuckled.

But soon there were no more pleasant moments in the lovely mission gardens. The little lame priest grew weaker. To get relief from the pain he spent most of the time pressing his chest against the rough boards of the bed. Sometimes he sat on the floor where the strong arms of his native friends supported him.

Early in the afternoon of August 28 the exhausted Father Serra sat on the chair to ease his breathing. He asked for a cup of broth. Soon after, he turned to Father Palóu.

"It is siesta time," he said softly. "Now let us go to rest." He had not slept for over thirty hours because of the pain.

He lay down on his bed. Father Palóu covered him with the remaining half of his blanket and placed the crucifix on his breast. A short time later Father Palóu looked in on his sick friend.

"He is having a good sleep," he thought. Then he realized that it was a different kind of sleep — one that Father Serra would not wake from. Father Palóu's eyes filled with tears.

All that day and the next, church bells tolled and cannons boomed out the sad message about "Bendito Padre," as Father Serra was fondly known. Weeping natives from miles around Carmel came to pay their respects to the little lame priest.

They touched his face and hands with their rosary beads. They placed wreaths of yellow, purple, and pink wildflowers on his coffin. They remembered these were his favorites, especially the pink Castilian rose.

In spite of two guards at the coffin, a number of the neophytes cut tiny pieces of cloth from Father Serra's habit and snipped pieces of his hair.

The next day, August 29, 1784, Father Palóu held funeral services for his dearest friend. Hundreds attended in honor of the brave son of Saint Francis. Then his body was lowered into an opening in the floor of the church next to the altar.

The long journey of the little Franciscan missionary had ended!

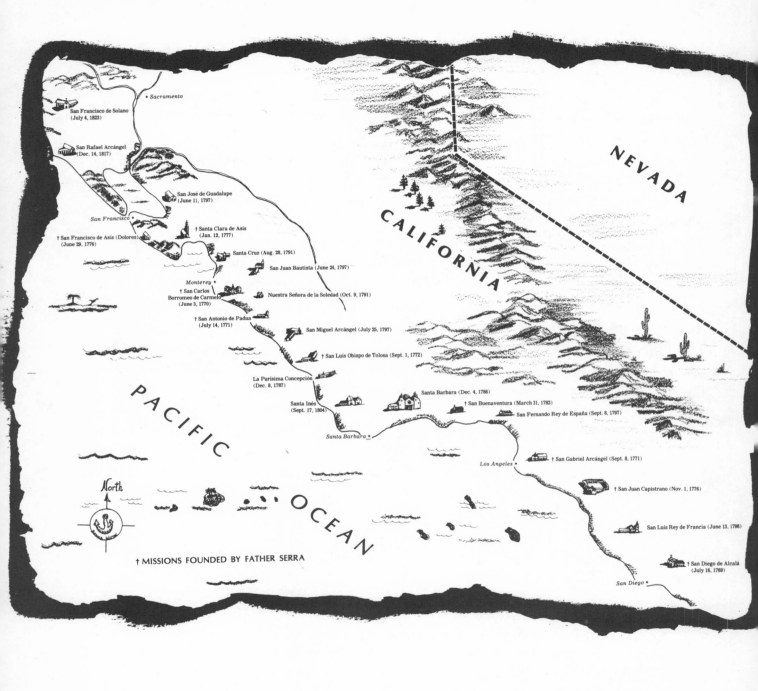

San Francisco de Solano
(July 4, 1823)

• Sacramento

San Rafael Arcángel
(Dec. 14, 1817)

NEVADA

CALIFORNIA

San José de Guadalupe
(June 11, 1797)

San Francisco

† Santa Clara de Asis
(Jan. 12, 1777)

† San Francisco de Asis (Dolores)
(June 29, 1776)

Santa Cruz (Aug. 28, 1791)

San Juan Bautista (June 24, 1797)

Monterey •

† San Carlos
Borromeo de Carmelo
(June 3, 1770)

Nuestra Señora de la Soledad (Oct. 9, 1791)

† San Antonio de Padua
(July 14, 1771)

San Miguel Arcángel (July 25, 1797)

† San Luis Obispo de Tolosa (Sept. 1, 1772)

La Purísima Concepción
(Dec. 8, 1787)

Santa Inés
(Sept. 17, 1804)

Santa Barbara (Dec. 4, 1786)

† San Buenaventura (March 31, 1782)

San Fernando Rey de España (Sept. 8, 1797)

Santa Barbara •

PACIFIC

Los Angeles •

† San Gabriel Arcángel (Sept. 8, 1771)

† San Juan Capistrano (Nov. 1, 1776)

San Luís Rey de Francia (June 13, 1798)

North

OCEAN

† San Diego de Alcalá
(July 16, 1769)

San Diego •

† MISSIONS FOUNDED BY FATHER SERRA

The Unofficial "Saint"

Father Junípero Serra's influence in California would never end. Over two hundred years later his way of life is evident everywhere.

Farms and ranches cover the state of California. It is the top agricultural state in the country. Some of its crops — particularly artichokes, olives, almonds, and figs — are grown almost solely in California. These had their beginnings in Father Serra's lush mission gardens and orchards. He also introduced oranges, apricots, and grapes to the dry desert lands. But first he taught the secret of irrigation to his neophytes, California's original farmers.

Moreover, his mission ranches, run by native vaqueros, set the stage for California's great livestock industry. Among the nation's states it ranks second in value of livestock.

In the fifteen years he traveled on "The Golden Chain," 1769-1784, the little lame padre founded nine missions, two pueblos, and four presidios. Four important West Coast cities grew from missions or presidios under Father Serra — San Diego, Los Angeles, San Jose, and San Francisco.

He called the route he followed on the mission chain El Camino Real, "The Royal Highway" (or "The King's Highway"). It still bears that name. Today, railroads and freeways are built close by the now heavily traveled road. One has only to close one's eyes and imagine how it once was — a narrow, tangled deer trail trod by silent moccasined feet, then widened and stamped down by the heavy boots of Captain Gaspar de Portolá and his men. But the slight, gray-robed friar limping behind them would leave not only the footprints of his dusty sandals but also imprint his goals and dreams upon this great new land.

To honor this tireless Franciscan missionary his name has been given to schools, museums, streets, highways, and ships. His statue is found in many places in California. The one most visited is at the State Capitol in Sacramento. Even more important is the one in Statuary Hall in Washington, D.C. There each state has contributed statues of two of its favorite sons or daughters. California chose to honor Father Junípero Serra with one of its two statues. (The other statue is that of Thomas S. King, a Unitarian minister.)

Many recognize that California's history might have been very different had it not been for the little priest's faith and courage. If he had abandoned his missions, as some tried to convince him to do, California would not have been settled until many years later. And the coming of civilization, culture, and the Christian religion would have been delayed.

Some in California as well as other parts of the world call Father Serra a "saint." They hope that the Catholic Church will make him one officially in the near future. He has already achieved two of three steps in this direction. The Church has declared him venerable and beatified. When Father Serra is canonized, then the third step will have been completed.

But for now he is California's unofficial "saint" — the little lame padre who always chose to go forward and never turn back.

Glossary

A Boy's Dream

- *espinagada:* spicy eel and vegetable pie.
- *Franciscan:* a person who belongs to the religious order founded by Saint Francis of Assisi.
- *friar:* a member of a religious order.
- *friary:* the friars' home.
- *Saint Francis:* founder of the Franciscan order.
- *New World:* the continents of North and South America.
- *native:* a person born in a particular place or country.
- *missionary:* a religious person who travels away from home to tell people about God.
- *Majorca:* a Spanish island in the western Mediterranean Sea; the largest of the Balearic Islands.

Farewell to Petra

- *neophyte:* a person who is a new member of a church or religion; a newly baptized church member.
- *feast day:* a religious holiday celebrating a special church event with prayers, rejoicing, and feasting.

"You're Too Short!"

- *canon:* a clergyman on the staff of a cathedral or other large church.
- *novice:* one who has entered a religious house for training and is on probation.

- *lectern:* a high reading desk near the altar; it holds the priest's religious books.
- *hymnal:* a book containing religious songs.
- *Brother:* a member of a men's religious order who eventually may or may not become a priest, depending on his calling.
- *Fray:* the Spanish word meaning "Brother."
- *vow of poverty:* a promise to God never to own any material possessions.
- *priest:* a person who is granted the holy right to perform religious duties in a church.
- *mission:* a place where missionaries live while performing religious and charitable work among the natives of that region; it is more than a church; it has rooms to sleep, eat, and work in.
- *Father Guardian:* the highest ranking priest in charge of a cathedral or college of a religious order.

Perilous Journeys

- *indemnity:* the act of making up for some loss or injury.

Attempted Murder

- *Mass:* the church service in the Catholic and Episcopal churches.
- *Sierra Gorda:* an untamed part of Mexico located in the heart of the jagged mountain range called the Sierra Madre.
- *mystery play:* a religious acting out of incidents in the life, death, and resurrection of Christ.
- *Nativity play:* a religious play acting out the incidents relating to the birth of Christ.
- *habit:* the dress of a religious person; sometimes a gown or robe.
- *beam:* a large, long heavy piece of timber used in building.

"Always Go Forward — Never Turn Back"

- *presidente:* the Spanish word for the person who heads an organization of religious persons.
- *padre:* the Spanish word meaning a "Catholic priest or monk."
- *pueblo:* the Spanish word for "town."
- *altar:* a table or raised flat surface used by religious people in celebrating the church service; it

is at the front part of the church.

• *vestments:* colorful robes and gowns worn by priests during church services.

Dangerous Times Ahead

• *muleteer:* one who is in charge of the mules.

• *tallow:* animal fat that is melted and used to make soap and candles; the fat comes from cattle or sheep.

• *scurvy:* a sometimes fatal disease due to a diet lacking vitamin C; it causes bleeding and swollen gums, weakness, and anemia.

• *Christians:* those who believe in or belong to the religion of Jesus Christ.

• *tule:* large thick grasses growing in swampy lands.

• *patron saint:* a special saint of the Church to whose care a person, church, or place is dedicated.

Forward to Monterey

• *watch fire:* a fire lit in the wilderness and used as a signal to guide travelers to their destination.

• *musket:* a type of rifle that is reloaded with gunpowder after each shot.

• *presidio:* a fort or military outpost.

• *palisade:* a fence of pales (stakes) used for defense; a long, pointed stake set with others in a close row as a defense.

• *stockade:* a fencelike enclosure built for protection and made of strong stakes or posts placed upright in the ground.

Two Missions in Two Months!

• *incense:* the perfume and smoke coming from spices and tree gums when they are burned in religious ceremonies.

• *baptize:* to make someone a member of the Christian church by sprinkling or pouring holy water on the person.

• *idol:* a figure, sometimes carved of wood or stone, representing a god of a non-Christian religion.

- *reservoir:* a place where water is stored for future use.
- *grist mill:* a building in which grain is ground into flour.
- *adobe:* a type of clay earth from which unfired bricks are made.

Problems Everywhere!

- *colony:* a group of people transplanted from their mother country to another land but remaining under the control of the parent country.
- *gully:* a miniature valley or gorge excavated by running water.

The Chain Grows Longer

- *padre-presidente:* a Spanish term for the religious person who is the supreme head of a group of priests.
- *candelabra*: a large ornamental candlestick having several branches; it is sometimes made of silver or gold.
- *vessel:* a hollow utensil, sometimes made of silver or gold, that is used for holding liquid during the church service; also, another name for a boat or ship.
- *chapel:* a small open room next to the main altar; it contains a smaller altar where church services may be performed.
- *continent:* one of the seven large divisions of land on the globe; in this particular case it refers to the continent of North America.
- *Declaration of Independence:* a document in which the thirteen American colonies proclaimed their freedom from Britain; it was formally adopted by Congress on July 4, 1776.

"In California Is My Life"

- *courier:* a special messenger.
- *corral:* a pen or enclosure for confining animals; also, an enclosure for defense and security.
- *tega:* a roof tile; it is made from molded clay and baked in a kiln until it is deep red.
- *tortilla:* a thin round flat cake of ground-up corn or wheat flour and baked in a flat hot pan.
- *reed:* a tall bamboo-like grass.
- *stocks:* a frame of timber with holes for the feet and hands to confine offenders by way of punishment.
- *shackles:* leg chains.

- *Christianize:* to make a person a Christian.
- *medicine man:* a native who is thought to have special powers to heal the sick.

The Journey Ends

- *rush:* a tall plant often with a hollow stem; used in plaiting mats.
- *crucifix:* a cross, a Christian emblem.
- *siesta:* the Spanish word for "a short rest at midday."
- *Bendito Padre:* the Spanish words meaning "Blessed Father."
- *rosary beads:* a string of beads used in counting prayers while reciting a special Catholic prayer called the Rosary.

The Unofficial "Saint"

- *irrigation:* supplying land with water by using canals or aqueducts to carry the water from a river or stream.
- *vaquero:* the Spanish word for "cowboy."
- *civilization:* the state of being no longer in a wild or savage state.
- *culture:* the customs, arts, and ways of life in a nation or people.
- *saint:* a holy, religious person who has been canonized by the Catholic Church.
- *venerable:* the state of a religious person that is the first step of three to becoming a saint of the Church; this person has been proven to have led a life of religious accomplishment.
- *beatified:* the second step in attaining sainthood; it agrees that the candidate has been responsible for a miracle; moreover, he is entitled to public religious honor and to be called "Blessed."
- *canonized:* the third and final step in the Church declaring a person a "saint"; usually it is done after it has been proved that he or she has performed a second miracle.

Bibliography

Breath of Sun (Life in Early California as Told by a Chumash Indian, Fernando Librado, to John P. Harrington). Malki Museum Press; Morango Indian Reservation; Banning, Calif.; 1979.

The Missions of California: A Legacy of Genocide. R. Costa; American Indian Historical Society; San Francisco, Calif.; 1986. (The effect of the mission system on the native American of California.)

Mediterranean Island Hopping — The Spanish Islands. Dane Facaros and Michael Pauls; Regnery Gateway; Chicago, Ill.; 1981.

Encyclopedia Americana (International Edition). Grolier, Inc.; Danbury, Conn.; 1986. (See sections on California and Majorca.)

Encyclopedia Britannica. Benton Publisher; Chicago, Ill., and London, England; 1986. (See sections on California and Majorca.)

California Facts (Flying the Colors Series). Clements Research, Inc.; Dallas, Tex.; 1985.

Your Washington and Mine. Charles Latimer; Scribner's; New York, N.Y.; 1924. (National Hall of Statuary — Father Serra's statue.)

Diary of Fra Junípero Serra, O.F.M. Being an Account of His Journey from Loreto to San Diego: March 28 to June 30, 1769. Franciscan Missionaries of Mary; North Providence, R.I.; 1935.

Founding of the First California Mission Under the Spiritual Guidance of Junípero Serra. Francisco Palóu; translated by Douglas Watson; Nueva California Press; San Francisco, Calif.; 1934.

Sally and Father Serra. Sarah Duque; Tabor Publishing; Valencia, Calif.; 1988.

Entry of Serra's Death (In the Book of the Dead at Mission San Carlos, Carmel), as written by Fray Francisco Palóu on August 28, 1784; translated by Lawton Kennedy et al.; Nueva California Press; San Francisco, Calif.; 1934.

Junípero Serra. Don De Nevi and Noel Francis Moholy; Harper & Row; San Francisco, Calif.; 1985.

Life and Times of Fray Junípero Serra (2 vols.). Maynard J. Geiger, O.F.M.; Academy of American Franciscan History; Washington, D.C.; 1959.

Mission San Carlos Borromeo. Fray Zephyrin Engelhardt; Franciscan Fathers; Mission Santa Barbara; Santa Barbara, Calif.; 1934.

The California Missions: A Pictorial History. Sunset-Lane Publishing Co.; Menlo Park, Calif.; revised edition, 1979.

Father Junípero Serra. Ivy May Bolton; Julian Messner, Div. of Simon & Schuster, Inc.; New York, N.Y.; 1952.

California's Father Serra. Sally Duque; Binfords & Mort Publishing; Portland, Ore.; 1958.

Father Junípero Serra, the Traveling Missionary. Linda Lyngheim; Langtry Publications; Van Nuys, Calif.; 1986.

Fray Junípero Serra and the California Conquest. Winifred Esther Wise; Scribner's; New York, N.Y.; 1967.

The Mission Bell. Leo Politi; Scribner's; New York, N.Y.; 1953.

The California Missions. Hans W. Hannan; Doubleday & Co., Inc., Div. of Bertelsman, Inc.; New York, N.Y.; 1966.

Live Again Our Mission Past. George Kusha and Barbara Linse; Educational Book Distributors; Larkspur, Calif.; 1984.

In His Footsteps — The Life Journey of Junípero Serra. Gertrude Ann Sullivan, B.V.M.; Catholic Conference, Division of Education; Sacramento, Calif.; 1984.

Whispers Along the Mission Trail. Gail Faber and Michelle Lasagna; Magpie Publications; Alamo, Calif.; 1986.

The Indians and the California Missions. Linda Lyngheim; Langtry Publications; Van Nuys, Calif.; 1984.

The California Missions. Edited by Ralph B. Wright; California Missions Trails Association, Ltd.; Arroyo Grande, Calif.; 1983; Hubert A. and Martha Lowman — publishers and distributors.

California Missions (The Earliest Series of Views — Made in 1856): The Journal and Drawings of Henry Miller. Bellerophon Books; Santa Barbara, Calif.; 1985.

The Story of the California Missions (book, tape, and filmstrip). Chevron School Broadcast; San Francisco, Calif.; 1982.

Mission Tales — Stories of the Historic California Missions. Helen M. Roberts; Stanford University Press; Stanford, Calif.; 1948.

The Padres' Garden. Clarence A. Marcy, M.A.; Harr Wagner Publishing Co.; San Francisco, Calif.; 1932.

The Royal Road. Charlie May Simon; E. P. Dutton and Co., Div. of NAL/Penguin; New York, N.Y.; 1948.

Tales Tolled by the Mission Bells. Jessie R. Kistler; Research Publishing Co.; Los Angeles, Calif.; 1947.

California Stepping-Stones. Robert Kingery Buell; Stanford University Press; Stanford, Calif.; 1948.

In addition to these books, research was accomplished through the use of four California State social studies textbooks; the many pamphlets, booklets, and tour guide brochures purchased at the twenty-one missions; and numerous newspaper and magazine clippings about Father Serra.

California's Golden Chain of Missions

Although Father Junípero Serra founded only the first nine missions, other Franciscan missionaries later established twelve more. These twenty-one missions offered hospitality to travelers along El Camino Real for over five hundred miles of Alta California.

Father Serra's missions:

San Diego de Alcalá / July 16, 1769

San Antonio de Padua / July 14, 1771

San Luís Obispo de Tolosa / September 1, 1772

San Juan Capistrano / November 1, 1776

San Buenaventura / March 31, 1782

San Carlos Borromeo de Carmelo / June 3, 1770

San Gabriel Arcángel / September 8, 1771

San Francisco de Asís / June 29, 1776

Santa Clara de Asís / January 12, 1777

Later missions

Santa Barbara / December 4, 1786

Santa Cruz / August 28, 1791

San José de Guadalupe / June 11, 1797

San Miguel Arcángel / July 25, 1797

San Luís Rey de Francia / June 13, 1798

San Rafael Arcángel / December 14, 1817

La Purísima Concepcíon / December 8, 1787

Nuestra Señora de la Soledad / October 9, 1791

San Juan Bautista / June 24, 1797

San Fernando Rey de España / September 8, 1797

Santa Inés / September 17, 1804

San Francisco de Solano / July 4, 1823